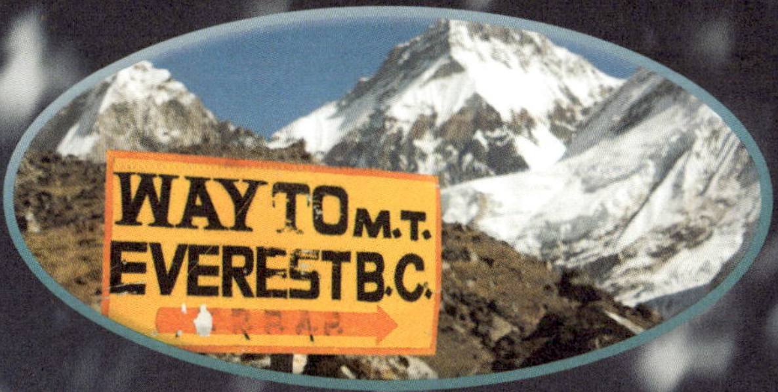
WAY TO M.T.
EVEREST B.C.

© iStock.com/DanielPrudek

© iStock.com/fotoVoyager

© iStock.com/Koonyongyut

© iStock.com/diamirstudio

© iStock.com/sihasakprachum

© iStock.com/RafalBelzowski

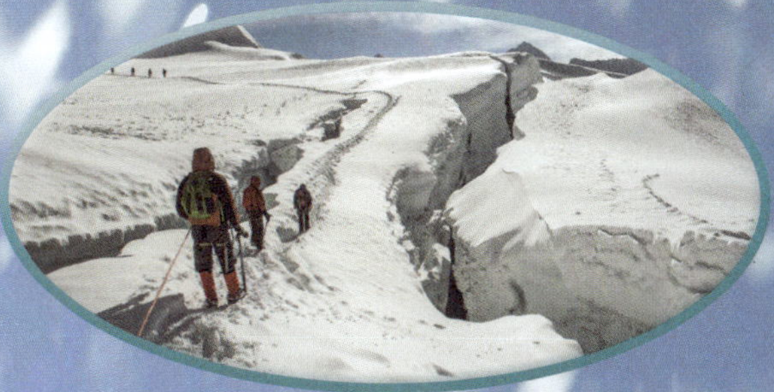

© iStock.com/sihasakprachum

Congratulations!
You have achieved the ultimate challenge!

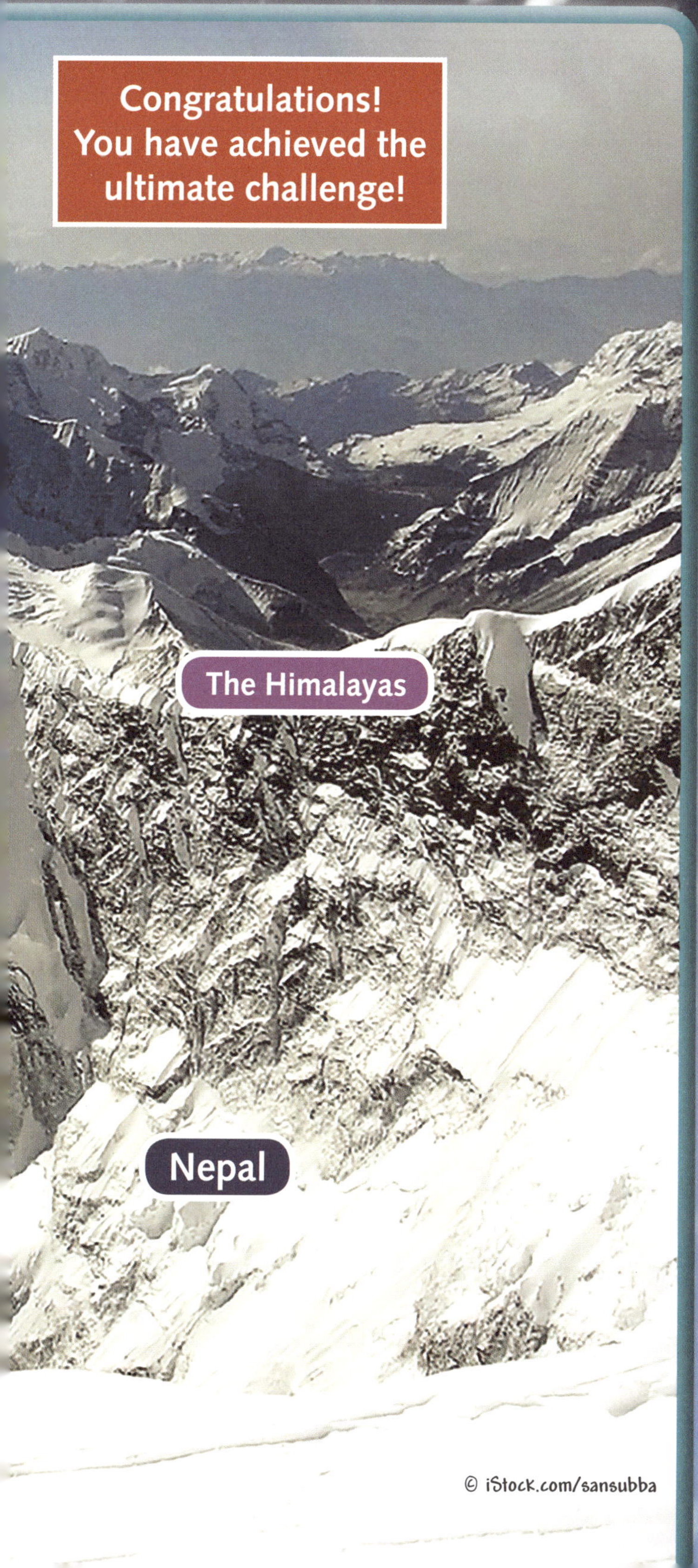
The Himalayas
Nepal

© iStock.com/sansubba

© iStock.com/loops7 [background snowstorm photo]

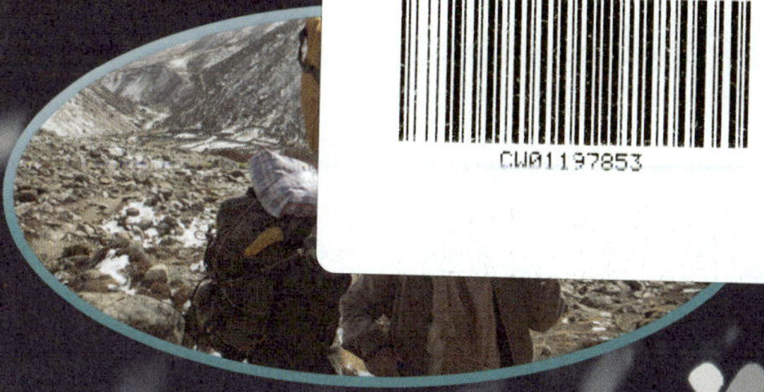

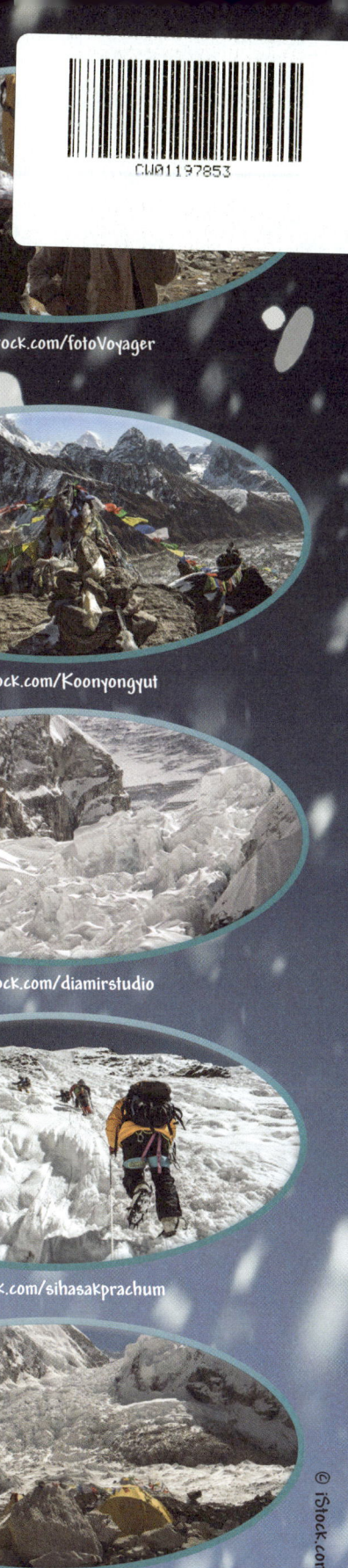

Pharaoh on the Phone

By William

Read the words.

Set 1 (10 words)	Set 2 (20 words)	Set 3 (20 words)	Set 4 (20 words)	Set 5 (20 words)
pharaoh	phrase	physique	diaphragm	photographic
phone	paragraph	pheasant	phobia	euphemism
nephew	physical	alphabet	prophecies	photocopies
trophy	graph	emphatic	spherical	catastrophic
elephant	sphere	physical	paragraphs	triumphantly
phenomenal	phase	emphasis	orphanage	apostrophe
Joseph	graphs	metaphor	graphical	catastrophe
photograph	phlegm	triumphant	hemispheres	amphibians
telephoto	phew	atmosphere	pharmacist	physically
triumph	hyphen	pharmacy	euphoric	atmospheric
10 words so far	dolphin	emphasise	autograph	phenomenon
	prophet	microphone	saxophone	biographical
	phonic	telephone	blasphemy	alphabetical
	orphan	prophecy	geography	claustrophobia
	phantom	hemisphere	philosopher	geographical
	phony	megaphone	hyphenated	phenomenally
	earphones	epitaph	photocopy	photosynthesis
	physics	physicist	biography	metamorphosis
	pamphlet	photographs	amphibian	autobiography
	phobic	decipher	emphasises	autobiographical
	30 words so far	50 words so far	70 words so far	90 words so far

One Minute Wonders

	up to 39 Sparkling	40–49 Glowing	50–59 Burning	60–69 Sizzling	70+ Red hot!
Score/Date					
Score/Date					

4

Read the story then draw the picture.

The Pharaoh was on the phone telling his nephew about the trophy he had won for his elephant training.
"That's phenomenal!" screeched Joseph. "I will come and take a photograph of you with my new telephoto lens. What a triumph!"

Practise writing.

Build your word power.

Well done!
ch (sh)
ent
si (sh)
ough
ant
s (zh)
ible
ci (sh)
able
ti (sh)
ph

Brilliant! You are off!

Mount Everest is a phenomenal mountain, situated in the Himalayas in the northern hemisphere. You have been training for two years, including how to use ice-screws, snow belays, crampons and ice axes. You have tried out all your equipment in snow and ice conditions, often practising with thick gloves on, as frostbite usually affects your hands. It will be the toughest physical challenge of all and you are hoping to achieve this personal triumph without any catastrophes!

tious tient tial tiate

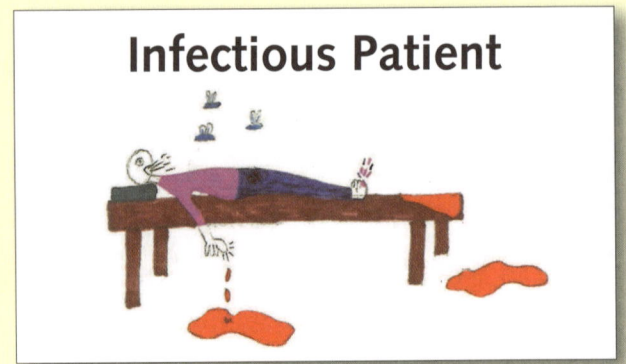

Infectious Patient

By Charlie

Read the words.

Set 1 (10 words)	Set 2 (15 words)	Set 3 (15 words)	Set 4 (15 words)
ambitious	spatial	impartial	unessential
infectious	partial	cautiously	repetitious
patient	martial	contentious	impatiently
confidentially	patience	deferential	essentially
potentially	scrumptious	superstitious	unambitious
nutritious	initial	ostentatious	substantially
substantial	fictitious	confidential	flirtatiously
initially	potential	initiate	ambitiously
cautious	impatient	influential	insubstantial
essential	flirtatious	residential	negotiating
10 words so far	palatial	negotiate	ostentatiously
	torrential	presidential	differentiate
	patiently	preferential	surreptitiously
	pretentious	surreptitious	non-residential
	sequential	conscientious	differentiation
	25 words so far	40 words so far	55 words so far

One Minute Wonders

	up to 39 Sparkling	40–49 Glowing	50–59 Burning	60–69 Sizzling	70+ Red hot!
Score/Date					
Score/Date					

6

Read the story then draw the picture.

The ambitious young doctor was determined to cure his infectious patient.
"I must tell you, confidentially, that your disease is potentially fatal. Therefore, you must eat only nutritious food and take these splendidly substantial tablets!" he declared.
Initially, the patient was cautious, but finally agreed that the tablets were probably essential.

Practise writing.

Build your word power.

Well done!
ch (sh)
ent
si (sh)
ough
ant
s (zh)
ible
ci (sh)
able
ti (sh)
ph

Brilliant! You made it to the next stage!

You cannot be too ambitious, so it is essential to acclimatise to avoid altitude sickness. Therefore, you start by trekking for ten days to the South Base Camp at 5364 metres with Sherpas who carry most of your equipment. Sherpas help climbers reach the top of Everest as a job in order to support their families. Two Sherpas have climbed Everest 21 times! Often you must be patient and wait for the right conditions before climbing, as bad weather is potentially lethal.

7

able
ably

Capable Cat

By Rosie

Read the words.

Set 1 (9 words)	Set 2 (20 words)	Set 3 (20 words)	Set 4 (20 words)	Set 5 (20 words)
capable	available	comfortably	disposable	considerably
probably	probable	miserably	profitable	unreasonably
miserable	payable	tolerably	comparable	considerable
inevitable	changeable	fashionably	excitable	uncomfortable
reliably	breakable	forgettable	repairable	invaluable
suitable	lovable	adorable	questionable	unsustainable
manageable	fixable	desirable	untreatable	undesirable
adaptable	bendable	acceptable	unthinkable	inevitably
regrettably	solvable	enjoyable	amiable	unavailable
	curable	exchangeable	respectable	unbelievably
9 words so far	treatable	unsuitable	unbearable	unbelievable
	valuable	incapable	sustainable	unmistakable
	vulnerable	noticeable	presumably	inconceivable
	tolerable	variable	irritably	understandable
	memorable	predictably	adorably	unavailable
	comfortable	achievable	predictably	unprofitable
	fashionable	remarkable	knowledgeably	recognisable
	reasonable	dependable	intolerable	unforgettable
	favourable	believable	improbable	disagreeable
	reasonably	affordable	unreasonable	understandably
	29 words so far	49 words so far	69 words so far	89 words so far

One Minute Wonders

	up to 39 Sparkling	40–49 Glowing	50–59 Burning	60–69 Sizzling	70+ Red hot!
Score/Date					
Score/Date					

8

Read the poem then draw the picture.

The Capable Cat sat down and thought
That sadly he was probably right:
Those miserable mice with their inevitable lice
Could not be reliably caught.

But he set up a trap in a suitable patch
And hoped that his plan was manageable
But the adaptable mice worked it out in a trice
So regrettably, there was not one to catch!

Practise writing.

Build your word power.

Well done!
ch (sh)
ent
si (sh)
ough
ant
s (zh)
ible
ci (sh)
able
ti (sh)
ph

Brilliant! You made it to the next stage!

You pitch your tent and spend a week at Base Camp before starting. You wonder at the considerable amount of rubbish lying around. Sleeping at Base Camp is not comfortable, as breathing is difficult and the glacier creeks underneath you! The views all around are truly remarkable. On one day you have a headache and suffer from dizziness. Are you getting altitude sickness? Fortunately, you recover and don't have to go down the mountain to rest. That would have been miserable.

cian ciate
cious cial
cient

Atrocious Magician

By Alex

Read the words.

Set 1 (11 words)	Set 2 (20 words)	Set 3 (20 words)	Set 4 (20 words)
atrocious	ancient	capacious	inefficient
magician	conscious	voracious	avaricious
electrician	especially	tenacious	ungraciously
crucial	appreciate	malicious	insufficient
optician	social	audacious	dietician
official	racial	vivacious	politician
technician	facial	provincial	associate
special	vicious	proficient	unconsciously
gracious	precious	deficient	vivaciously
sufficient	spacious	commercial	multiracial
unconscious	luscious	auspicious	suspiciously
11 words so far	glacial	fallacious	voraciously
	musician	subconscious	maliciously
	ferocious	graciously	atrociously
	delicious	unofficial	commercially
	judicial	artificial	statistician
	beautician	beneficial	mathematician
	financial	superficial	inefficiently
	suspicious	antisocial	insufficiently
	efficient	inauspicious	officiating
	31 words so far	51 words so far	71 words so far

	up to 39 Sparkling	40–49 Glowing	50–59 Burning	60–69 Sizzling	70+ Red hot!
Score/Date					
Score/Date					

Read the story then draw the picture.

The atrocious magician was not an electrician and made a crucial error: he did not visit the optician nor call an official technician to help him wire his special box. When his gracious assistant stepped inside it, the electric shock was sufficient to send her unconscious!

Practise writing.

Build your word power.

Brilliant! You made it to the next stage!

Mid-May is the crucial 'summit window': the precious time when the jet stream moves north. The weather is calmer and warm enough to reach the top. However, you make sure you have sufficient clothing: long underwear, shell pants and light top; a shell jacket and a warm jacket for rests; leather gloves, special sunglasses, a headlamp and a thermal hat to protect against the vicious cold. Hypothermia can kill in only 30 minutes, as your body can lose heat rapidly.

Well done!
ch (sh)
ent
si (sh)
ough
ant
s (zh)
ible
ci (sh)
able
ti (sh)
ph

Sizzling Syllables!  1

Read the syllables.

Six syllable types

Closed	amp	esk	emp	olt	upt	ift	act	int	onk	ult
Open	fla	re	slo	le	mo	pe	twi	la	me	tro
Evil e	ane	ete	ile	ome	ule	ape	epe	ise	oze	upe
Vowel	bai	way	fee	rea	goa	low	goo	few	cue	lew
-r	spar	ster	orst	thir	der	spur	snar	blur	plor	squir
-le	-zle	-tle	-ple	-kle	-fle	-dle	-cle	-ble	-gle	-sle

Got it? ☐

Conquer Everest patterns

phew	tial	ciate	phin	tiate	pho
cian	cient	phys	tious	able	phar
ably	sphere	able	cious	phant	cient
phen	tience	cial	seph	tient	proph

Got it? ☐

Prefixes and suffixes

-ing	mis-	re-	dis-	-al	im-	-ful
-ment	inter-	de-	-est	non-	-y	-ed
pre-	-ness	-ity	pro-	-ly	il-	un-
-en	sub-	-er	-less	semi-	-able	be-
trans-	-ous	-ic	fore-	non-	over-	under-

Got it? ☐

12

Fiery Phrases! 1

Pharaoh on the Phone

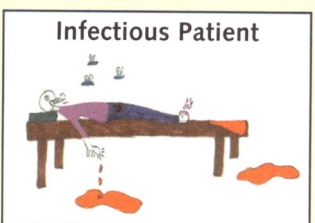
Infectious Patient

Capable Cat

Atrocious Magician

Read the phrases.

Set 1	Set 2	Set 3
feed the elephant	the cat moved cautiously	a remarkable person
photograph the dolphin	shows great potential	it wasn't affordable
what a triumph	negotiate a deal	wear disposable gloves
learn the alphabet	don't be superstitious	achievable grades
help the orphans	an impatient teacher	an irritable man
a great atmosphere	a confidential letter	riding for disabled people
pass me the microphone	an infectious laugh	a reliable car
where is the pharmacy	martial arts	the ferocious tiger
my nephew won the trophy	racial equality	a vivacious girl
the Earth is a sphere	rooms available	a multiracial town
the phantom of the opera	variable weather	a suspicious package
a ghostly phenomenon	beyond reasonable doubt	his artificial leg
use a telephoto lens	wear comfortable shoes	visit the optician
such a catastrophe	such fashionable clothes	glacial features
please use paragraphs	a memorable event	a great musician
an excellent phrase	hide your valuables	the financial agreement
geographical features	a vulnerable animal	I appreciate your help
remember the apostrophe	the heat was intolerable	a facial expression
newts are amphibians	considerably larger	what a malicious trick
infectious patient	a nutritious snack	atrocious manners
20 phrases	20 phrases	20 phrases

	up to 29 Sparkling	30–39 Glowing	40–49 Burning	50–59 Sizzling	60+ Red hot!
Score/Date					
Score/Date					

13

ible
ibly

Incredibly Flexible Flora

By Flora

Read the words.

Set 1 (8 words)	Set 2 (20 words)	Set 3 (20 words)	Set 4 (20 words)	Set 5 (20 words)
terribly	possible	visibly	inaudible	indestructible
flexible	terrible	illegible	contemptible	irresistible
incredible	impossible	collectible	infallible	irreversible
sensible	horrible	detectible	implausible	indefensible
responsible	visible	constructible	irascible	irresponsibly
horribly	edible	eligible	inedible	indigestible
impossibly	legible	admissible	collapsible	irresponsible
invisible	credible	indelible	invisibly	inaccessible
8 words so far	gullible	defensible	incredibly	irresistibly
	audible	distractible	combustible	imperceptible
	fallible	illegibly	inaudibly	inexhaustible
	feasible	inedible	susceptible	comprehensible
	plausible	exhaustible	accessible	indivisible
	crucible	destructible	submersible	inadmissible
	forcible	divisible	reducible	inflexibility
	legibly	digestible	inflexible	incomprehensible
	possibly	reversible	submergible	accessibility
	sensibly	invincible	responsibly	invisibility
	forcibly	convertible	irrepressible	responsibility
	audibly	incredibly	incompatible	impossibility
	28 words so far	48 words so far	68 words so far	88 words so far

up to 39 Sparkling	40–49 Glowing	50–59 Burning	60–69 Sizzling	70+ Red hot!
Score/Date				
Score/Date				

Read the story then draw the picture.

Flora was terribly clever; she was so flexible that she could bend into positions that were incredible. Luckily, we were far too sensible and responsible to try and coil our bodies into such horribly twisted shapes.
"That one is impossibly difficult!" we cried as her head became almost invisible.

Practise writing.

Build your word power.

Brilliant! You made it to the next stage!

First, you must cross the Khumbu Icefall. This is an incredible 600 metre climb on a moving glacier, with aluminium ladders to take you across the terrible, frighteningly deep crevasses. It's only possible if you start before sunrise to minimise the movement of the glacier as the sun rises and heats it up. Thus at 3am on 8 April you eat a quick, almost indigestible, breakfast. You must eat as you will be burning about 10,000 calories a day – double that once on the summit.

Well done!
ch (sh)
ent
si (sh)
ough
ant
s (zh)
ible
ci (sh)
able
ti (sh)
ph

sure
sion

Vision of Treasure

By Edward

Read the words.

Set 1 (8 words)	Set 2 (18 words)	Set 3 (18 words)	Set 4 (18 words)
television	**measure**	measurement	provisions
erosion	**decision**	precision	displeasure
explosion	occasion	provision	composure
division	leisure	intrusion	remeasure
revision	pleasure	exposure	measuring
envisioned	vision	inclusion	leisurely
explosions	closure	persuasion	treasurer
treasure	fusion	transfusion	cohesion
8 words so far	treasured	delusion	collisions
	invasion	derision	pleasurable
	collision	diffusion	indecision
	conclusion	seclusion	supervision
	confusion	infusion	occasional
	evasion	allusion	provisional
	enclosure	effusion	disillusioned
	exclusion	corrosion	illusionary
	illusion	measurements	occasionally
	treasuring	disclosure	provisionally
	26 words so far	44 words so far	62 words so far

One Minute Wonders

	up to 39 Sparkling	40–49 Glowing	50–59 Burning	60–69 Sizzling	70+ Red hot!
Score/Date					
Score/Date					

16

Read the story then draw the picture.

On television, there was a programme showing that erosion nearby had caused an explosion and some precious gems were thrown up into the air like a firework! My division revision was totally forgotten while I envisioned explosions of treasure happening in *my* garden!

Practise writing.

Build your word power.

Brilliant! You made it to the next stage!

At Crampon Point, it's crampons on and you start to climb, sometimes at 60 degrees. Breathing is difficult. The exposure when stepping, rung by rung, over the first deep crevasse makes your heart pound. Everyone must keep their composure. Later, you reach the Popcorn Field, an area where there are loud crashes as pieces of serac break off. On occasions, climbers have been hit; the noises can cause confusion and people often cover their heads with their hands in fright.

Well done!

| ch (sh) |
| ent |
| si (sh) |
| ough |
| ant |
| s (zh) |
| ible |
| ci (sh) |
| able |
| ti (sh) |
| ph |

17

ant ance ancy

The Important Ant
By Marianna

Read the words.

Set 1 (9 words)	Set 2 (20 words)	Set 3 (20 words)	Set 4 (20 words)	Set 5 (20 words)
elephant	**pleasant**	balance	applicant	insurance
defiant	**distant**	distance	adamant	maintenance
arrogant	**substance**	nuisance	hesitant	disturbance
giant	**significant**	fragrance	confidant	circumstance
important	restaurant	instance	stimulant	assistance
unpleasant	relevant	guidance	ignorant	tenancy
elegant	instant	clearance	buoyancy	infancy
brilliant	infant	consultant	truancy	extravagance
jubilantly	pregnant	defendant	observant	unimportant
9 words so far	constant	reluctant	observance	irrelevant
	tenant	immigrant	resemblance	inhabitant
	vacant	attendant	expectant	extravagant
	merchant	assistant	triumphant	deodorant
	servant	descendant	tolerance	occupancy
	dormant	vacancy	pregnancy	decongestant
	truant	occupant	ignorance	accountancy
	buoyant	tolerant	importance	redundancy
	blatant	redundant	acceptance	consultancy
	tyrant	emigrant	allowance	hesitancy
	fragrant	reluctance	radiant	insignificant
	29 words so far	49 words so far	69 words so far	89 words so far

	up to 39 Sparkling	40–49 Glowing	50–59 Burning	60–69 Sizzling	70+ Red hot!
Score/Date					
Score/Date					

18

Read the story then draw the picture.

"Out of my way!" said the elephant.
"No!" said the defiant ant. "Don't be so arrogant. I may not be a giant but I'm important too."
"I'm sorry. I was being unpleasant," the elegant elephant replied. "Let me take you for a ride."
"How brilliant! Thank you," said the ant jubilantly.

Practise writing.

Build your word power.

Well done!
ch (sh)
ent
si (sh)
ough
ant
s (zh)
ible
ci (sh)
able
ti (sh)
ph

Brilliant! You made it to the next stage!

Three hours on, you take an important break on a flat section known as the football field, and take off your 9 kilogram load. An unpleasant icy wind makes you put on your down jacket. Five more hours of ladders and steep climbs, followed by an hour of flat snow before you reach Camp 1, covered with yellow tents. Once there, you feel triumphant; the view is brilliant! You drink a lot as dehydration can lead to headaches, frostbite and confusion.

ough

O U Greedy Hamster

By Lucia

Read the words.

Set 1 (7 words)	Set 2 (13 words)	Set 3 (15 words)	Set 4 (9 words)
enough	thought	though	bough
thought	ought	although	plough
trough	bought	dough	ploughed
rough	fought	doughnut	ploughing
tough	nought	doughy	drought
coughed	wrought		
through	brought	thorough	cough
	thoughtful	borough	coughed
7 words so far	thoughtless	thoroughly	coughing
	thoughtlessly	thoroughness	trough
	thoughtfully		
			44 words so far
		enough	
	through	rough	
		tough	
	hiccough	chough	
		roughly	
	20 words so far	rougher	
		35 words so far	

One Minute Wonders

	up to 39 Sparkling	40–49 Glowing	50–59 Burning	60–69 Sizzling	70+ Red hot!
Score/Date					
Score/Date					

Read the story then draw the picture.

The greedy hamster was full up. He had definitely eaten enough.
In fact, he thought he had eaten too much. His trough was totally empty and the rough, tough skin on his little nose was covered in muck.
He coughed and spluttered, "Oh dear! Will I fit through the tunnel to my cosy den?"

Practise writing.

Build your word power.

Well done!
ch (sh)
ent
si (sh)
ough
ant
s (zh)
ible
ci (sh)
able
ti (sh)
ph

Brilliant! You made it to the next stage!

On 10 April it's back to Base Camp to allow your body to recover. On 12 April you set off to Camp 1 again. This requires mental toughness, as it is such a physical challenge, although your body has acclimatised somewhat. Three hours more to Camp 2, roped up to fellow climbers as the thin snow bridges can collapse at any moment. You thought you would never make it. The temperature reaches 38°C as the sun emerges. Phew! Suddenly, the clouds return and you plough your way through falling snow all the way up to Camp 2.

 Sizzling Syllables!

Read the syllables.

Run Australia review

ceil	fasten	rear	ware	fair	crumb	earn
gnash	earl	chem	ney	neer	earth	ceive
mare	leer	ield	gore	bey	pare	teer
hear	dair	plore	knock	fear	lore	orch

Got it? ☐

New Conquer Everest patterns

sure	ant	sion	ought	ibly	sion
cough	ssion	ible	sure	ancy	through

Got it? ☐

All Conquer Everest so far

pher	tial	able	cian	phew	ciate	sion
cious	phan	sure	tious	ought	pho	tience
tient	cial	cough	tiate	ably	phys	sure
ible	enough	phant	sion	through	cient	ibly

Got it? ☐

Fiery Phrases! 2

Incredibly Flexible Flora

Vision of Treasure

The Important Ant

O U Greedy Hamster

Read the phrases.

Set 1	Set 2	Set 3
terrible weather	she needs supervision	she was adamant
sensible shoes	a tremendous explosion	there is a vacancy
an incredible result	on this occasion	truancy is a problem
irresistible cakes	a terrible intrusion	he was feeling confident
a convertible car	nothing on television	he used a buoyancy aid
her writing is illegible	to my confusion	I ought to go
the team is invincible	the extreme soil erosion	he brought a friend
could you possibly help	a tourist invasion	ploughing the fields
the food was indigestible	measure the distance	a terrible drought
the rules were inflexible	with such precision	such a hacking cough
she was visibly shaken	a brilliant restaurant	I've had enough
please be sensible	he was a tolerant tenant	the rough seas
he got it terribly wrong	a blatant lie	the meat was really tough
the music was inaudible	it's very unimportant	we love doughnuts
it's a pleasure	she returned triumphant	through the tunnel
he showed his displeasure	such fragrant deodorant	the old water trough
the lion's enclosure	a complete tyrant	thoroughly tired of it
treasured memories	don't feel hesitant	a bad case of hiccoughs
at a leisurely pace	in an instant	we need to toughen up
I came to the conclusion	that's totally irrelevant	such a thoughtful man
20 phrases	20 phrases	20 phrases

	up to 29 Sparkling	30–39 Glowing	40–49 Burning	50–59 Sizzling	60+ Red hot!
Score/Date					
Score/Date					

sion
ssion

Tension in the Mansion

By Libby

Read the words.

Set 1 (10 words)	Set 2 (20 words)	Set 3 (20 words)	Set 4 (20 words)
discussion	possession	emission	concession
procession	profession	depression	suspension
diversion	passion	succession	regression
mansion	version	repression	recession
permission	mission	obsession	accession
expression	session	submission	digression
impression	pension	immersion	transgression
comprehension	sessions	conversion	oppression
tension	percussion	transmission	compression
aggression	excursion	dimensions	submersion
10 words so far	confession	concussion	aspersion
	progression	suppression	aversion
	compassion	commission	dimensional
	extension	omission	pensionable
	expansion	inversion	repossession
	admission	reversion	intermission
	dimension	expulsion	repercussion
	convulsion	subversion	compassionate
	revulsion	propulsion	impressionist
	confessions	pensioner	impressionistic
	30 words so far	50 words so far	70 words so far

	up to 39 Sparkling	40–49 Glowing	50–59 Burning	60–69 Sizzling	70+ Red hot!
Score/Date					
Score/Date					

24

Read the story then draw the picture.

After some discussion, the carnival procession took a diversion right through the local mansion without permission from the owner. His expression was quite a sight! We had the impression that this event was beyond his comprehension. You could feel the tension as he kept his aggression under control.

Practise writing.

Build your word power.

Well done!
ch (sh)
ent
si (sh)
ough
ant
s (zh)
ible
ci (sh)
able
ti (sh)
ph

Brilliant! You made it to the next stage!

Three days at Camp 2 (6400 metres) before returning to Base Camp to rest up. On 21 April, you're climbing to Camp 3 by fixed rope (Everest has 10,000 metres of rope!). This difficult three-hour climb leaves a deep impression on you. Each rope is 60 metres long and you must unclip your carabiner and jumar at each junction – difficult in thick gloves. Your progression up the mountain is arduous; you have to kick your crampon into the hard ice every step of the way, and you arrive totally drained.

ent ence ency

Silent Student

By Joshua

Read the words.

Set 1 (10 words)	Set 2 (20 words)	Set 3 (20 words)	Set 4 (20 words)	Set 5 (20 words)
adolescent	**present**	absent	decency	violently
student	**content**	silence	evidence	indifference
silent	**moment**	defence	existence	circumference
intelligent	**prevent**	sentence	consequence	obedient
excellent	**different**	absence	incidence	apparently
apparent	**permanent**	sequence	innocence	obedience
disobedient	**influence**	offence	fluency	incompetence
experiment	**independent**	presence	currency	experience
current	accident	violent	frequency	dependency
compliments	frequent	difference	sediment	convenient
10 words so far	government	reference	confidence	presidency
	parliament	violence	dependent	independence
	environment	incident	president	adolescence
	torrent	ornament	excellence	intelligence
	recent	instrument	dependence	residency
	client	element	residence	convenience
	advent	confident	impatience	inconvenient
	crescent	resident	permanence	disobedience
	decent	evident	frequently	inexperience
	fluent	innocent	currently	interdependence
	30 words so far	50 words so far	70 words so far	90 words so far

	up to 39 Sparkling	40–49 Glowing	50–59 Burning	60–69 Sizzling	70+ Red hot!
Score/Date					
Score/Date					

26

Read the story then draw the picture.

The adolescent student was silent most of the time, despite being very intelligent and an excellent violinist. One day, for no apparent reason, she was very disobedient and tried out an experiment with an electric current. Oh boy! Her hair received no compliments after that!

Practise writing.

Build your word power.

Well done!
ch (sh)
ent
si (sh)
ough
ant
s (zh)
ible
ci (sh)
able
ti (sh)
ph

Brilliant! You made it to the next stage!

10

4 May: First summit attempt. From Camp 3 onwards, you are dependent on bottled oxygen to help you breathe. The climbing is not technically difficult here, but doing anything at 8000 metres is gruelling. Reaching the tents, you eat and rest for several hours, hoping for clement weather. At 9pm, with headlamps on, you set off with your Sherpa. It is a frightening, steep and incredibly long climb in darkness. You must make frequent stops as teams of climbers queue to reach the summit.

ch (sh)

The Chic Chef

By Cecilia

Read the words.

Set 1 (10 words)	Set 2 (13 words)	Set 3 (13 words)	Set 4 (13 words)
Michelle	machine	creches	Chicago
chic	chute	chicane	chivalry
chef	niche	chagrin	chaperone
chiffon	cache	Cheryl	charlatan
champagne	creche	chassis	chauvinist
quiches	gauche	charades	ricochet
chalet	brochure	chevron	chandelier
chauffeur	cliche	gouache	nonchalant
trebuchet	crochet	moustache	Michigan
cachet	charade	Charlotte	marchioness
10 words so far	chamois	machete	chauvinism
	fuchsia	parachute	machinery
	sachet	crocheting	nonchalantly
	23 words so far	36 words so far	49 words so far

One Minute Wonders

up to 39 Sparkling	40–49 Glowing	50–59 Burning	60–69 Sizzling	70+ Red hot!
Score/Date				
Score/Date				

28

Read the story then draw the picture.

Michelle was a chic chef. Dressed in chiffon and sipping champagne, she sliced quiches in her chalet that the chauffeur fired across to her from a trebuchet! What cachet she had!

Practise writing.

Build your word power.

Brilliant! You've done it!

At 'the Balcony', you rest, eat, drink and replace your oxygen canister. Then it's an extremely cold climb along a terrifying knife-edge ridge, with ice chutes on either side. The Hillary Step is the final rock wall. You watch your Sherpa guide climb the 15 metre crack with machine efficiency and then force your exhausted body to follow. Finally, you stand among the prayer flags marking the top of the world! You cry as you pose for pictures on the 10 square metre summit with your Sherpa guide. If only you could parachute down for some celebratory champagne!

Well done!
ch (sh)
ent
si (sh)
ough
ant
s (zh)
ible
ci (sh)
able
ti (sh)
ph

29

Sizzling Syllables! ③

Read the syllables.

New *Conquer Everest* patterns

| ant | chiff | ssion | cham | ence | ency |
| ent | ency | ancy | ance | chal | chic |

Got it? ☐

***Conquer Everest* mix-up**

phen	tial	ence	chal	sure	ssion
ency	phys	ible	cial	able	phon
cian	pho	tious	sure	ent	phe
ibly	sion	ciate	seph	tiate	chic
ably	chiff	ant	cham	ancy	sion
phew	tient	cient	cious	phin	phib

Got it? ☐

All *WordBlaze*

ry	eep	oad	ait	sure	ick
ibly	uff	ant	cian	brow	tient
orce	tious	low	ture	ace	skim
ssion	due	airn	ieve	ent	grou
irm	oes	ency	awk	gest	igh
ver	drea	toon	cial	sheer	ciate
tience	ible	proph	ool	fare	udge
ley	oist	ives	mech	ence	ceil
otch	vore	sion	able	guin	cer
ancy	tion	hoy	gaun	wor	cious

Got it? ☐

30

Fiery Phrases! 3

Tension in the Mansion

Silent Student

The Chic Chef

Read the phrases. Do you remember all the spelling patterns you have learnt so far?

Set 1	Set 2	Set 3
the latest version	there is an accident	faulty machinery
show some compassion	very inconvenient	the silk parachute
she made a great impression	I need some foreign currency	a complete charlatan
what's your profession	that was an intelligent comment	the bullet ricocheted off
mission impossible	the dog is obedient	her strict chaperone
an act of aggression	it was a violent argument	the creche facilities
a total obsession	care for the environment	the weapons cache
traffic diversion	thank you for the compliment	bright fuchsia pink
go on an excursion	that is not very convenient	geographical information
tension was mounting	he is an adolescent	he advanced cautiously
great comprehension	it was a silent evening	particularly noticeable
we had a discussion	his excellency the president	insufficient supplies
we don't need possessions	he is incompetent	don't be gullible
may I have your permission	a niche market	the triumphant tyrant
he plays percussion	his bushy moustache	a thorough investigation
an excellent result	a sachet of medicine	a passion for sport
frequent interruptions	he is a chauvinist	read with fluency
that looks very different	a glittering chandelier	off to Chicago
she spoke with confidence	some holiday brochures	you are observant
unwrap your present	the car's chassis	revision is important
20 phrases	20 phrases	20 phrases

	up to 29 Sparkling	30–39 Glowing	40–49 Burning	50–59 Sizzling	60+ Red hot!
Score/Date					
Score/Date					

Blazing Extras

Read the words.

Psychic Sara

Silent p

By Anastasia

psychic	pneumatic
psychiatry	pneumonia
psychology	receipt
psychiatrist	psalm
psychiatric	pseudonym
psychological	pterodactyl

y in the middle

The Crystal Pyramid

By Mali

A Nylon Python

By Clare

rhythm	pyramid	rhyme	syphon
system	syllable	style	hydrogen
symbol	mystery	stye	dynamo
myth	synagogue	python	asylum
gym	synonym	cycle	dynamic
Egypt	symphony	tyrant	hyena
crystal	abysmal	hyphen	hygienic
cymbal	hypnotic	hygiene	hydration
abyss	mythical	nylon	paralysed
gypsy	synchronise	Lycra	analyse
rhythmic	symbolism	typist	paralyse
symptom	symmetrical	enzyme	rehydrate
typical	mysterious	pylon	carbohydrate
tympani	rhythmically	cyclist	tyrannical
symmetry	mysteriously	cyclone	dehydration

32

Be Active!

By William

v at the end needs e

give	furtive	aggressive	addictive	conclusive	unforgiving
live	massive	negative	fugitive	forgiveness	competitive
active	passive	repulsive	deceptive	actively	inoffensive
motive	positive	offensive	exclusive	decorative	indecisive
captive	creative	relative	excessive	positively	inconclusive
native	adjective	decisive	impulsive	hyperactive	creativity
forgive	sensitive	talkative	obsessive	captivity	communicative
festive	expensive	secretive	primitive	secretively	uncommunicative

The Neon Alien

By Seb

Split vowels

dial	create	burial	creation	diaphragm	intuition
trial	triumph	media	hideous	deviance	cooperate
diary	fluent	trivial	genuine	comedian	coordinate
liar	chaos	phobia	reimburse	material	coincidence
giant	diet	denial	helium	civilian	coordination
fluid	bias	genial	defiant	bacteria	cooperation
dual	violet	tibia	reliant	biology	claustrophobia
quiet	violent	deviate	pliable	aviation	coincidental
client	aerial	dialect	chaotic	defiantly	antibiotic

 White Hot Wonder!

Read the words.

Set 1	Set 2	Set 3	Set 4
terrible	brochure	chaperone	machinery
comprehension	available	incredibly	efficient
paragraph	enclosure	hemisphere	suspension
apparent	essential	extravagant	ambitious
especially	pleasant	adorably	hesitancy
unpleasant	visible	bought	supervision
thorough	triumph	ferocious	currency
patient	drought	confidence	catastrophe
fought	ancient	superstitious	irresponsibly
miserable	possession	obsession	chassis
erosion	excellent	audible	procession
experiment	confidential	apostrophe	appreciate
incredible	significant	occasion	tolerance
physical	intelligent	truancy	scrumptious
expression	reasonable	delicious	dormant
arrogant	legibly	unbearably	forcibly
probably	although	version	atmosphere
thoughtless	chef	frequency	conclusion
cautious	emphasise	nutritious	obedient
decision	expansion	moustache	unmistakable
20 words	20 words	20 words	20 words

Beat your time!

Set 1	Set 2	Sets 1 and 2

Set 3	Set 4	Sets 3 and 4